TABLE OF CONTENTS

INTRODUCTION

Welcome to the World of Cake Pops! Have you ever indulged in a sweet treat that's not only delicious but also irresistibly cute? In that case, you're in for a treat because we're about to take you on an adventure into the wondrous world of cake pops. These delectable confections are the result of a harmonious union of cake and artistic skill, and throughout this book, you'll learn the tricks of the trade for making them with panache and delicacy.

What makes cake pops so beloved, you might wonder? It's their ability to bring a smile to your face with every bite. Their delightful size and endless possibilities for customization make them perfect for all occasions, from birthday celebrations to casual gatherings. Whether you're a seasoned baker or a novice in the kitchen, cake pops are accessible to all, offering a canvas for creative expression.

Beyond their aesthetic charm, cake pops offer a taste that's hard to resist. The fusion of moist cake, luscious frosting, and a delectable coating of your choice, be it chocolate, candy melts, or icing, creates a flavor explosion that's truly exceptional. They're not just a dessert; they're an experience!

In this comprehensive cake pops recipe book, we've curated a delectable collection of over 70 cake pop recipes that span the spectrum of taste and creativity. Whether you're a professional pastry chef or someone simply looking for a fun and flavorful project, there's something here for everyone.

From timeless classics like Classic Chocolate Cake Pops and Red Velvet Love Bites to exotic creations such as Matcha Green Tea Zen Pops and Mexican Churro Dulce Pops, you'll find a recipe for every palate and occasion. We've even included options for those with dietary restrictions or seeking healthier alternatives, what else could you possibly wish for?

This book is not just a recipe collection; it's your gateway to mastering the art of cake pops. Inside, you'll discover essential techniques, tips for success, innovative design ideas, and solutions to common challenges. Whether you're a seasoned cake pop connoisseur or taking your first steps in the world of baking, this book promises to be your trusty companion.

So, let's embark on this sweet adventure together. Ready to craft, decorate, and savor these bite-sized wonders? Let's dive into the world of cake pops, where flavor meets artistry, one pop at a time. Your family and friends will be impressed!

A Brief History of Cake Pops

Cake pops have a fascinating origin that can be traced back to the creative minds of bakers and dessert enthusiasts. While their exact inception is debated, it's widely acknowledged that cake pops gained substantial popularity in the early 21st century, thanks to creative bakers and pioneers. These culinary visionaries transformed simple cake crumbs and frosting into miniature, edible masterpieces. Originally, cake pops were cherished for their whimsical appearance and portability, making them perfect for parties, weddings, and special events. Over the years, their popularity has soared, evolving from charming novelties to essential staples in the world of desserts.

The origins of cake pops are a captivating blend of creativity, resourcefulness, and culinary evolution. While the precise birthplace and date of cake pops remain a subject of debate, their emergence can be traced back to innovative bakers and dessert enthusiasts who transformed humble ingredients into bite-sized confections of joy.

One of the earliest manifestations of cake pops can be found in the frugality of generations past. In an era when minimizing food waste was a necessity, bakers sought inventive ways to repurpose leftover cake scraps. These scraps, often considered remnants or imperfections, were crumbled, and blended with frosting to create a malleable mixture. This mixture could then be shaped into small, round, or conical forms, resembling lollipops. These early iterations were a testament to the culinary ingenuity of their time.

While the idea of turning cake scraps into delightful confections was born out of necessity, it didn't take long for cake pops to transition from thrift-inspired creations to artistic expressions. Creative bakers and home cooks began to realize the potential of cake pops as a canvas for their culinary imagination.

As cake pops gained popularity, they became not only a delectable treat but also a whimsical and versatile medium for edible art. The 21st century saw an explosion of interest in cake pops, largely due to the efforts of pioneering bakers and creative entrepreneurs who brought them into the limelight. These early adopters began to experiment with flavors, shapes, and designs, elevating cake pops from mere leftovers to cherished centerpieces on special occasions.

The enchanting visual appeal of cake pops, with their colorful coatings, intricate decorations, and playful themes, played a significant role in their meteoric rise. They became the stars of dessert tables at weddings, baby showers, birthday parties, and even corporate events. Their small size made them ideal for portion control, and their portability made them a hit at food festivals and fairs.

Today, cake pops have transcended their humble beginnings and earned their place in the pantheon of beloved desserts. They remain a symbol of creativity and a testament to the ever-evolving world of culinary artistry. As you explore the recipes in this book and embark on your own cake pop adventures, you're joining a rich tradition of innovation that has transformed cake scraps into tiny, delectable masterpieces that bring joy to people of all ages.

ESSENTIAL EQUIPMENT, INGREDIENTS AND TECHNICES

Welcome to the heart of cake pop creation! Let's dive deep into the building blocks of crafting perfect cake pops. Just like any craft, having the right tools, quality ingredients, and mastering essential techniques is key to success. Whether you're a seasoned baker or a newcomer to the world of cake pops, these fundamentals will be your guiding stars.

The Must-Have Tools

Having the right tools is like having a well-organized toolbox for a skilled craftsman. These essential tools are your allies in crafting the perfect cake pops, ensuring they not only taste amazing but also look stunning. Let's explore the must-have equipment that will elevate your cake pop game.

The very essence of cake pops are the cake pop sticks. These slender sticks turn a simple cake ball into a lollipop-inspired masterpiece. Choose sticks that are sturdy, food-safe, and long enough to hold your cake pops comfortably. Standard lengths range from 4 to 6 inches, but you can find longer ones for a more dramatic effect. Wooden or paper sticks are popular options, and they are available in various colors to match your theme.

Molds and scoops are among the must have tools as well. Consistency is key in cake pop crafting, and molds and scoops are your secret weapons for achieving it. Silicone molds designed specifically for cake pops come in

12

various shapes, including spheres, hearts, and stars. They help you create uniformly sized cake pop balls with ease. Scoops, on the other hand, come in different sizes, allowing you to portion out the perfect amount of cake mixture for each pop.

For that flawlessly smooth and glossy coating on your cake pops, you'll need a melting pot or a microwave-safe bowl. These are essential for melting chocolate, candy melts, or icing. Look for options with a spout for easy pouring and precise dipping. Keeping the coating at the right temperature is crucial, so choose a pot or bowl that can be used with a double boiler or a microwave.

While not strictly essential, decorative accessories can take your cake pops to the next level. Think of items like edible sprinkles, glitter, or edible ink pens for drawing intricate designs. Luster dust, edible pearls, and food coloring gels add a touch of glamour. These tools allow you to express your creativity and make your cake pops stand out.

For more intricate designs and fine detailing, disposable decorating bags and a variety of decorating tips come in handy. These tools allow you to pipe designs, create patterns, and add textural elements to your cake pops. A set of different-sized tips will offer versatility in your decorating endeavors. Moreover, after dipping your cake pops in coating, they need a place to dry without smudging or losing their shape. A drying rack or foam block is invaluable for this purpose. Look for a rack with a non-stick surface, as it makes removing the pops after they've dried much easier.

In addition to drying racks or foam blocks, cooling racks are essential for cooling your freshly baked cake layers. Proper cooling is essential for achieving the ideal texture for your cake crumbles. These racks allow air to circulate around the cake, preventing excess moisture and ensuring your cake pops aren't too mushy.

For melting chocolate, candy melts, or icing, a double boiler or microwave-safe bowls are indispensable. They allow for gentle, even melting without the risk of burning your coating. A double boiler consists of a lower pot filled with simmering water and an upper bowl or pan for melting your ingredients. If you prefer using a microwave, opt for microwave-safe bowls with a spout for precise pouring.

Another important tool is surely a kitchen scale. It might not be the first tool that comes to mind, but it's incredibly useful for measuring ingredients with precision. Achieving the right cake-to-frosting ratio is crucial for the texture and taste of your cake pops. A kitchen scale ensures accuracy, especially when dealing with specific weights of ingredients.

To maintain the perfect temperature for your coating, a candy thermometer or an instant-read thermometer is indispensable. Different coatings require specific temperatures for dipping, and a thermometer helps you achieve that perfect, glossy finish without overheating or underheating the mixture.

While not a tangible tool, having ample freezer or refrigerator space is essential for setting your cake pops. These spaces are crucial for firming up your cake pops after dipping, ensuring the coating sets perfectly, and your cake pops maintain their shape and appearance.

Last but not least, decorative stands and displays. Though not strictly essential, they add a touch of sophistication to your cake pop presentation. These come in various styles and themes to match your occasion. They're perfect for creating stunning displays at parties, weddings, or other events. With the right stand, your cake pops become both a delightful treat and a visual centerpiece.

Remember that your tools are your allies in creating miniature works of edible art. Investing in quality equipment can make your cake pop journey smoother and more enjoyable. With the right tools, you'll be well-prepared to shape, dip, and decorate your way to a dazzling array of cake pops that will impress everyone lucky enough to savor them.

Essential Ingredients

In this chapter, we will embark on a culinary journey to explore the key ingredients that form the foundation of every delectable cake pop. From the cake base to the binding agents and coating options, understanding and selecting the right ingredients is essential for crafting cake pops that are both delicious and visually appealing.

Cake Base

One of the most timeless bases is surely classic vanilla. It offers a mild, pleasant flavor that serves as a versatile canvas for various frostings and coatings. The simplicity of vanilla cake allows it to pair well with a wide range of flavors, making it an excellent choice for those who prefer a neutral base.

Another popular option is a chocolate base. Chocolate cake is a beloved choice for cake pops, especially among chocolate enthusiasts. Its deep, cocoa-rich flavor provides a robust foundation for your pops. The rich and indulgent taste of chocolate cake pairs wonderfully with various coatings, creating a delightful chocolate experience. Besides, depending on what you like, you may use darker and richer chocolate, children's favorite milk chocolate or even white chocolate options. The possibilities are almost endless nowadays!

You may also use red velvet cake as a base, which is known for its subtle cocoa undertones and vibrant red color. It's a visually striking choice for cake pops, and its mild cocoa flavor harmonizes beautifully with cream cheese frosting. Red velvet cake pops are perfect for adding a touch of elegance to your dessert table.

If you're seeking a refreshing and zesty flavor, lemon zest cake is an excellent option. The citrusy twist in this cake base adds a burst of brightness and a unique flavor profile to your cake pops, making them ideal for spring and summer gatherings. You may also try a lime zest cake, or similar citrusy flavors for a more playful version.

Strawberry shortcake cake pops offer another delicate and fruity flavor. The use of strawberry cake base creates a refreshing and sweet taste, making them a perfect choice for spring and summer events. You may try and prepare the cake base also based on other fruity options if you desire.

For those looking to infuse their cake pops with a delightful crunch, consider using crushed cookies within the cake base. Cookies 'n Cream cake pops offer a satisfying texture and the classic cookies and cream flavor that many adore. You may even add some crushed or ground nuts if desired.

Are you familiar with the Funfetti base? Adding a dash of whimsy and a splash of color to your cake pops is the name of the game. Because it contains multicolored sprinkles that are baked into the cake, it generates a delightfully childlike and aesthetically pleasing dessert that is ideal for birthdays, festivities, and parties aimed at children.

Last but not least, the double chocolate fudge cake. It's an absolute dream come true with its robust and luscious chocolate taste. Combine it with chocolate or dark chocolate coatings to create a chocolate experience that is impossible to resist.

How to: Making an Easy Cake Base

Some of us are used to baking cakes, others bake them only on occasion. We are sure many of you have some great recipes up your sleeve, but for all of those who don't, we prepared a quick and easy step-by-step guide on how to easily prepare a base for a chocolate or vanilla cake, which you can transform into a fruity cake base if needed, along with some valuable tips and tricks.

You have to gather your ingredients first, many of which we can find in a basic pantry. For a basic cake, you'll need ingredients like flour, sugar, cocoa powder (for chocolate cake), baking powder, baking soda, salt, eggs, milk, vegetable oil (or butter), and vanilla extract. But what quantity of ingredients would you need? For a 9-inch round cake pan, you would need approximately 2 cups of flour, 1 to 1.5 cups of sugar (or to taste), ½ or 1 cup of butter or vegetable oil (butter for a richer flavor, oil for moisture), Eggs: 3 to 4 large eggs, 1 cup of liquid (usually milk), 1 to 1.5 tsps baking powder and ½ tsp baking soda, a pinch of salt and 1 or 2 tsps pure vanilla extract (or other extracts based on flavor, like cocoa powder, fruit extracts, etc.).

There is one easy rule: mix the dry ingredients (flour, sugar, cocoa powder, baking powder, baking soda, and a pinch of salt, etc.) in one bowl, and the wet ingredients (eggs, milk, butter, oil, vanilla extract, etc.) in another. Mixing the ingredients separately ensures even distribution in the batter, ensures even mixing and helps to remove lumps. Once you have both bowls ready, combine them together gradually and gently. Do not rush the process as lumps may occur. Mix until just combined. Overmixing can make the cake tough, so stop once there are no visible dry flour pockets.

For chocolate cake, stir in hot water to the batter until well combined. The hot water helps bloom the cocoa powder for a rich flavor. Don't worry; the batter will be thin. There is no need for this step for vanilla or other fruit type cakes.

Add the batter evenly to the cake pan (you can use two pans). Smooth the tops with a spatula. The base should be baked in an oven at recommended temperature (usually 350°F or 175°C), for about 25.35 minutes. Do not forget to grease and flour your cake pans before you put them in the oven or else the batter will stick.

Once baked, let the cakes cool in the pans for about 10 minutes. Then, run a knife along the edges to loosen them and remove them from the pans. Let the cakes cool completely on wire racks. You may either use the recipe to make an actual cake, or to crumble the cake for a cake pop recipe.

Tips & Tricks:

- Ensure your eggs, milk, and butter (if using) are at room temperature. This helps with even mixing and a better cake texture.
- Use dry measuring cups for dry ingredients and liquid measuring cups for wet ingredients. Level off excess with a flat edge for precise measurements.
- Mix until just combined to prevent overdeveloping gluten, which can make the cake tough.
- Prevent the cake from sticking to the pan by greasing it and dusting it with flour. You can also use parchment paper at the bottom.
- Ensure the cakes are completely cooled before frosting. Warm cakes can cause the frosting to melt and slide off.
- Use a toothpick to check if the cake is done. When it comes out clean (with a few crumbs), it's ready.
- Feel free to add additional flavors like coffee or citrus zest for a unique twist on your cake. For a Red Velvet Cake Base, add a touch of red food coloring and a touch of vinegar. For a fruit flavored base, add fruit puree (e.g., mashed bananas, applesauce, or pureed berries) or fruit extracts (e.g., lemon, orange, or raspberry) based on your desired flavor. The amount can vary but start with about ½ cup of puree or a few tsp of extract. Adjust to taste. Ensure that the fruit puree or extract is well-mixed into the batter for a consistent flavor.

How to: Chocolate Fudge Cake

This is the most popular cake option for many people that can bring your pops on another level. Let's see how you can transform your classic vanilla or chocolate cake recipe into a fudge cake!

As a base, prepare your basic cake batter ingredients and incorporate them well, to a point that you have a smooth batter. Now it's time to add some fudgy vibe to it.

For this step, you will need to combine half a cup of unsweetened cocoa powder, 1 cup chocolate (or dark chocolate) chips, half a cup of hot water, and instant coffee granules (if using). They are not necessary but will enhance the chocolate flavor. Stir until the chocolate has melted and the mixture is smooth. Add the fudge mixture to your basic cake batter and stir to combine.

Mix in half a cup of butter or oil until well incorporated. This adds moisture and richness to the fudge cake. Stir in two cups of granulated sugar (or to taste), followed by three eggs, one at a time. Mix well after each addition. Finally, add the pure vanilla extract (1 tsp or to taste) and stir to combine. Your batter is now ready and should suffice for a 9x13-inch baking pan.

Bake the batter in the preheated oven on 350°F for about 35-40 minutes. If you want to a toothpick test, you can, but is should not come out entirely clean, but rather with a few moist crumbs as the center of the cake. Be careful not to overbake, as fudge cake should be moist and slightly gooey.

Once cooled, it's ready to use for your cake pops. You can also eat it straight away If you can't resist.

Frosting and Binding Agents

There is a wide variety of choices available; thus, let's get right down to business and discuss the option of using cream cheese frosting. It has a tangy, somewhat sweet taste that goes particularly well with red velvet and carrot cake pops; therefore, we consider it to be our favorite flavoring option. Because of its smooth consistency, it is also an efficient binding agent, which enables the cake crumbs to maintain their original form.

Another adaptable alternative that is often utilized in the manufacturing of cake pops is icing made from buttercream. Because of its sugary and velvety texture, it works well with a diverse variety of cake bases. Not only does the buttercream improve the taste of the cake, but it also does an outstanding job of acting as a binding agent.

It is impossible to go wrong with a chocolate ganache when making chocolate-based cake pops. Chocolate ganache has a rich and velvety texture, and it offers a delicious contrast to lighter cake bases while also adding a layer of pure chocolate taste.

If, on the other hand, you are looking for something a little bit different, you may want to think about using flavored icing, such as almond, lemon, or hazelnut. Your cake pops will have a flavor that is both subtle and distinct when you use these flavored icings, which will enable you to experiment with a variety of flavor combinations.

How to: Making an Easy Frosting

We prepared a quick and easy step-by-step guide on how to easily prepare a basic frosting for your cake, which you can transform into a flavored frosting if needed, along with some valuable tips and tricks.

First, let's gather the essential ingredients. Ensure you have unsalted butter (or cream cheese for cream cheese frosting), confectioners' sugar (powdered sugar), milk or heavy cream, pure vanilla extract (or other desired flavorings), and a pinch of salt. For a basic recipe, you will need 1 cup (2 sticks) of unsalted butter, 4 cups of powdered sugar, 2 or 3 tbsps of milk or heavy cream, 1 tsp of vanilla extract (or other extracts, if using) and a pinch of salt.

Before you start, make sure that the butter is at rooms temperature. This way, the butter is easier to mix into a smooth frosting. If using cream cheese, it should also be at room temperature. Beat the butter (or cream cheese) until it's creamy and smooth, using an electric mixer. This usually takes 2-3 minutes.

Then, prepare the sugar. Use powdered sugar or stiff the confectioners' sugar to remove any lumps. Gradually add it to the butter mixture, one spoon at a time, while mixing on low setting. Sifting ensures your frosting will be smooth and free of sugar clumps.

Now it's the time to add all wet ingredients. You can adjust the amount of liquid for the consistency that you prefer. More liquid makes it thinner; less liquid makes it thicker. You may ask, why would we need to add a pinch of salt? Well, it enhances the flavor of the frosting. After adding all the ingredients, mix on low for a continuous 2 or 3 minutes, until the mixture is smooth and fluffy. You are ready to go!

Tips & Tricks:

- Add more sugar if you believe the frosting is thin, more liquid if too thick.
- Experiment with different flavorings or extracts for unique flavors.
- For colorful frosting, add food coloring in small amounts until you achieve the desired color. Add it gradually, drop by drop to avoid overcoloring.
- For Flavored Frostings, you can experiment with different extracts (e.g., almond, lemon, or orange) or fruit purees to create unique flavors.
- For Chocolate Frosting, add ½ to ¾ cup of unsweetened cocoa powder along with the sugar. You can also melt and cool 4-6 ounces of semi-sweet or bittersweet chocolate and add it to the frosting for a richer flavor.
- For Cream Cheese Frosting, replace one stick of butter with 8 ounces of cream cheese. The rest of the instructions remain the same!

- Taste the frosting as you go and adjust the sweetness or flavor to your liking.

How to: Chocolate Ganache

Chocolate Ganache is one of the most popular items that can bring your pops on another level. You may use it as a filling, frosting, cake layer, dip, spread, and topping. So, it's important to take a few quick steps on how to make it up your sleeve!

For a Ganache, you will need equal parts of heavy cream and high-quality chocolate. Th chocolate should be finely chopped. Alternatively, you can use chocolate drops. This way, it will melt quicker and evenly.

Heat the cream in a saucepan until it begins to simmer. You'll see small bubbles around the edges of the cream. Be careful not to let it boil or burn it, so heath in over lower heath and watch it carefully. Once hot, pour it over the chopped chocolate. Let it sit for 1-2 minutes, so that the chocolate begins to melt. Start stirring the mixture gently. Start from the center and move outward in small circles. Keep stirring until the chocolate is completely melted and the ganache is smooth and glossy.

Allow the ganache to cool to your desired consistency. For pouring over cake pops, it should be slightly warm. For spreading, filling, or piping, let it cool to room temperature.

Tips & Tricks:

- High-quality chocolate will make your ganache taste and look better.
- Avoid boiling the cream, as it can scorch the chocolate and affect the ganache's texture.
- Vigorous stirring can introduce air bubbles and make the ganache less smooth so do it slowly and gently.
- If your ganache is too thick, you can warm it slightly. If it's too thin, let it cool a bit longer.
- Experiment with flavored ganache by adding extracts (e.g., mint, orange), liquors (e.g., Grand Marnier, Amaretto), or spices (e.g., cinnamon).
- You can store leftover ganache in the refrigerator in a container or a Ziploc bag. Reheat it when needed.

Coatings

Among the cake pops coatings, chocolate is a classic choice. It provides a smooth and rich exterior with a timeless flavor. You can choose between dark, milk, or white chocolate, depending on your preference and the overall theme of your cake pops.

Dark chocolate provides an intense and slightly bitter cocoa flavor. It's an excellent choice for those who prefer a more sophisticated and less sweet coating. It pairs beautifully with a wide range of cake bases, from red velvet to double chocolate fudge. Milk chocolate on the other hand is known for its sweet and creamy taste. It's a crowd-pleaser, making it an ideal choice for cake pops that are served at children's parties or gatherings where a sweeter taste is preferred. Milk chocolate complements vanilla, funfetti, and cookies 'n cream cake pops exceptionally well. Another option is white chocolate that has a sweet, vanilla-like flavor and a creamy texture. It's an excellent option for those who want to create a visually striking contrast with dark or colorful cake pops. White chocolate pairs nicely with cake bases like strawberry shortcake or funfetti, as it allows their flavors to shine through.

Candy melts, also known as candy coating or confectionery coating, offer a rainbow of colors and a variety of flavors. They are formulated to melt smoothly and harden quickly, making them a popular choice for creating vibrant and themed cake pops. Candy melts have a sweet, vanilla flavor that's distinct from real chocolate. The advantages of candy melts include:

- A broad color palette for creating visually appealing cake pops to suit different themes or occasions.
- Quick and easy melting, with no need for tempering like real chocolate.
- A smooth, consistent texture for coating your cake pops.
- The ability to create intricate designs and shapes.

Icing is another coating option that offers a more delicate and subtle finish. While it's not as commonly used as chocolate or candy melts, it can be an excellent choice when you want the flavor of your cake base to shine through. Icing can be applied in various ways:

- Drizzling: Thin the icing to a pourable consistency and drizzle it over the cake pops. This method allows the cake's flavor to be front and center.

- Dipping: Dip the cake pops into the icing for a thin, smooth coating that enhances the cake's taste.

- Piping: Use a piping bag with a fine tip to create intricate designs or add textural elements to your cake pops.

Icing is perfect for creating an elegant, less sweet coating, and it's a great choice when you want to focus on the taste of the cake itself.

When selecting a coating for your cake pops, consider the flavor and visual appeal you want to achieve. Chocolate provides a rich and classic taste, candy melts offer vibrant colors and creativity, and icing emphasizes the cake's flavor. Experiment with different coatings to find the perfect match for your cake pops, and don't hesitate to mix and match coatings with various cake base flavors for a diverse and visually captivating display.

Basic Techniques

Now that we've explored the essential tools and ingredients, it's time to roll up our sleeves and get into the nitty-gritty of crafting perfect cake pops. Basic techniques are the building blocks of cake pop mastery. Let's dive into the step-by-step process and essential tips that will help you create cake pops that are not only delicious but also visually stunning.

Crumbling the Cake

The journey to crafting the perfect cake pop begins with baking your favorite cake. Once your cake is baked to perfection, allow it to cool completely. This step is essential as working with a fully cooled cake prevents excess moisture, which could lead to a mushy texture when crumbling.

Once your cake is cooled, it's time to crumble it. You can use a fork, your hands, or a food processor for this task. Gently break the cake into fine crumbs, ensuring that there are no large chunks left. The goal is to achieve a uniform consistency in the crumbled cake.

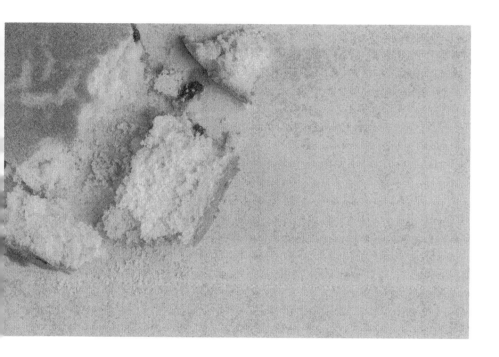

Mixing in the Frosting

After your cake crumble is prepared, it's time to select your frosting. Choosing the right frosting is a crucial step in crafting the perfect cake pop. Consider the flavor of your cake and select a frosting that complements it. Cream cheese frosting works wonderfully with red velvet, while buttercream is a versatile option that pairs well with many cake flavors.

Once prepared, add the frosting gradually to your cake crumbs. This step is essential to control the texture and consistency of your cake pop mixture. You want a mixture that can be molded into a ball without being too dry or too sticky. Begin with a 1:1 ratio (equal parts cake and frosting) and adjust as needed.

Carefully mix the frosting into the cake crumbs until the two are fully combined. The resulting mixture should have a uniform texture, with no visible streaks of frosting. Take your time with this step to ensure even distribution and a consistent taste throughout your cake pops.

Forming Cake Pops

When the base is prepared, dedicate your time to forming little cake pops. To create visually appealing and consistent cake pops, it's important to shape them uniformly. You can use your hands, silicone molds, or scoops for this step. Be sure to portion out the mixture into equally sized portions and then roll them into smooth cake pop balls. This not only enhances the visual appeal but also ensures even cooking.

To achieve that classic lollipop appearance, insert a cake pop stick into each cake ball. Prior to inserting the sticks, you can dip the tip of each stick into melted coating to act as a "glue." This helps the sticks adhere to the cake pops securely. Place the sticks in the center of each cake ball, ensuring they're stable and won't fall out during dipping.

Dipping in Coating

Depending on your preference and the flavor profile you want to achieve, you'll need to select the coating for your cake pops. Common choices include chocolate (dark, milk, or white), candy melts, and icing. It's essential to choose high-quality ingredients for the best results.

To melt the coating, you have several options. You can use a double boiler, a microwave, or a specialized melting pot. A double boiler involves placing a heatproof bowl over a pot of simmering water, ensuring that the bowl doesn't touch the water. Stir the coating until it melts evenly. In the microwave, use short bursts of heat, stirring between each burst to prevent overheating. Maintaining the proper temperature of your coating is essential. Different coatings have different ideal temperatures for dipping. Use a candy thermometer or an instant-read thermometer to monitor the temperature, and don't exceed it. Overheating can cause the coating to seize, resulting in a thick and unworkable consistency.

Once done, place the dipped cake pop upright in a drying rack or a foam block. This is where they will set and dry. Ensure that they're spaced apart to prevent any touching, which can lead to smudging. Allow the coating to harden before moving on to decoration. If your coating starts to thicken or harden during the dipping process, you can gently reheat it to achieve the desired consistency. Be cautious not to overheat, as this can affect the coating's texture. Another important tip is if you notice air bubbles in your coating, gently tap the cake pop while the coating is still wet to release them. Alternatively, you can use a toothpick or a scribe tool to pop any bubbles that form.

Once your cake pops are fully coated and decorated, store them in an airtight container at room temperature. Refrigeration is not recommended, as it can cause the coating to develop condensation and lose its sheen.

Dipping cake pops in coating is a crucial step in creating that enticing, glossy shell that encapsulates the delightful cake inside. Proper technique, attention to temperature, and a steady hand are essential for achieving a professional finish. The beast teacher is always experienced – learn from the failure and upgrade your technique to become better and better each time.

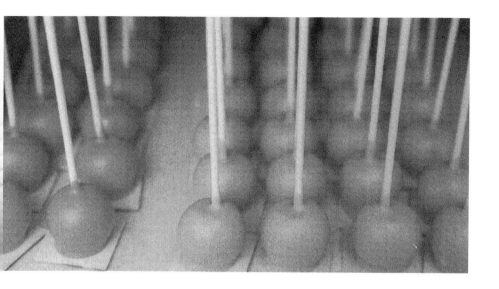

Decorating and Personalizing

Finally, it's time for decorations and personalizing your pops! It's the most fun activity to do. Invite a friend or do it with your family members so you can commonly decide on the themes and details.

For intricate designs, prepare a piping bag with a decorating tip of your choice. The choice of tip will depend on the design you want to create. For intricate details, choose fine tips, and for broader patterns, use larger ones. Fill the piping bag with melted coating or icing that's at the right consistency for your design.

Piping bags allow for precision and creativity. You can draw intricate patterns, write names or messages, and add fine details to your cake pops.

Use contrasting colors for a visually striking effect. For example, use white icing on dark chocolate-coated cake pops for an elegant contrast.

Then, add some edible accents! Edible sprinkles, glitter, and colored sugar crystals are fantastic choices for adding texture and sparkle to your cake pops. Experiment with different sizes, shapes, and colors to match the theme of your event or the flavor of your cake pops. Sprinkle them on while the coating is still wet to ensure they stick.

Luster dust is an additional inventive option to consider. It is a fantastic tool for generating a glittery and metallic appearance on your cake pops, which you may use to wow your guests. It comes in a variety of colors, including gold, silver, and pearl, among others. When applying the luster dust to your cake pops, use a brush that is clean and dry. This approach is ideal for producing a sheen that is both sophisticated and eye-catching. What about some pearls that you can eat? They are available in a wide range of dimensions and colors. You may use them to add an air of refinement to your cake pops by decorating them with them. But try to apply them while the coating is still wet so that they really stick to your pops well.

If the pearls do not intrigue you, you may go for edible gels. With them, you can create custom-colored coatings or intricate designs. You can mix them with melted white chocolate or icing to achieve the desired shades. These gels also work well for freehand painting on your cake pops. A similar option are also edible ink pens, which can be used for drawing fine details, intricate patterns, or writing personalized messages directly onto your cake pops. Besides, they are easy to use and add a personal touch to your creations, so why not try them out?

By exploring the world of decorating and personalizing, you can take your cake pops to a whole new level of creativity and presentation. Whether you're decorating for a special occasion, a themed party, or just for the joy of it, the art of personalizing your cake pops is a delightful and rewarding process that will impress your guests and tantalize their taste buds!

RECIPE BOOK

SIMPLE & CLASSIC CAKE POP RECIPES

Dark Chocolate Elegance

Making Time: 1.5 hours – 24 Cake Pops

Ingredients:
- *1 chocolate cake (homemade or store-bought)*
- *1 cup of chocolate frosting*
- *12 ounces of dark chocolate (for coating)*
- *Sprinkles or edible pearls for decoration*

Instructions:
- Crumble the chocolate cake into fine crumbs in a large bowl.
- Gradually add the chocolate frosting to the cake crumbs. Start with half a cup and adjust the amount as needed for the right consistency. Mix until well combined.
- Roll the mixture into uniform cake balls and insert cake pop sticks into each one.
- Melt the chocolate until runny and smooth, dipping the pops into it and allowing excess to drip off.
- Place the pops on a drying rack and immediately decorate with sprinkles or edible pearls.
- Allow the cake pops to set for about 15-20 minutes.

Chocolate Peanut Butter Delights

Making Time: 1.5 hours – 24 Cake Pops

Ingredients:
- *1 chocolate cake (homemade or store-bought)*
- *1 cup of chocolate frosting*
- *12 ounces of milk chocolate (for coating)*
- *½ cup of peanut butter*
- *Crushed peanuts for garnish*

Instructions:
- Crumble the chocolate cake into fine crumbs in a large bowl.

- Gradually add the chocolate frosting to the cake crumbs, starting with half a cup. Adjust the amount to achieve the desired consistency.
- Roll the mixture into uniform cake balls and insert cake pop sticks into each one.
- Melt the chocolate until runny and smooth, dipping the pops into it and allowing excess to drip off.
- Heat the peanut butter in a microwave until smooth and runny, drizzling it over the cake pops and immediately sprinkling them with crushed peanuts.
- Allow the cake pops to set for about 15-20 minutes.

Tangy Lemon Blueberry Pops

Making Time: 1.5 hours – 24 Cake Pops

Ingredients:
- *1 lemon cake with blueberries (homemade or store-bought)*
- *½ cup of lemon-flavored frosting*
- *12 ounces of white chocolate (for coating)*
- *Fresh blueberries and lemon zest for decoration*

Instructions:
- Crumble the lemon cake with blueberries into fine crumbs in a large bowl. Gradually add the lemon-flavored frosting to the cake crumbs, starting with half a cup. Adjust the amount for the desired consistency.
- Roll the mixture into uniform cake balls and insert cake pop sticks into each one.
- Melt the chocolate until runny and smooth, dipping the pops into it and allowing excess to drip off.
- While the coating is still wet, decorate the pops with a fresh blueberry and a sprinkle of lemon zest.
- Allow the cake pops to set for about 15-20 minutes.

Classic Red Velvet Sensation

Making Time: 1.5 hours – 24 Cake Pops

Ingredients:
- *1 red velvet cake (homemade or store-bought)*
- *1 cup of cream cheese frosting*
- *12 ounces of white chocolate (for coating)*
- *Red sanding sugar for decoration*

Instructions:
- Crumble the red velvet cake into fine crumbs in a large bowl.
- Gradually add the cream cheese frosting to the cake crumbs, starting with half a cup. Adjust the amount for the desired consistency.
- Roll the mixture into uniform cake balls and insert cake pop sticks into each one.
- Melt the chocolate until runny and smooth, dipping the pops into it and allowing excess to drip off.
- Immediately decorate them with red sanding sugar.
- Allow the cake pops to set for about 15-20 minutes.

Almond Amaretto Bliss

Making Time: 1.5 hours – 24 Cake Pops

Ingredients:
- *1 vanilla almond cake (homemade or store-bought)*
- *½ cup of almond-flavored frosting*
- *12 ounces of white chocolate (for coating)*
- *Slivered almonds for garnish*
- *2 tbsp of amaretto liqueur (optional)*

Instructions:
- Crumble the almond cake into fine crumbs in a large bowl.

- Gradually add the almond-flavored frosting to the cake crumbs. Start with half a cup and adjust for the desired consistency. Add amaretto liqueur if desired, for extra flavor.
- Roll the mixture into uniform cake balls and insert cake pop sticks into each one.
- Melt the chocolate until runny and smooth, dipping the pops into it and allowing excess to drip off.
- While still wet, sprinkle slivered almonds on top of each cake pop, then allow them to set for 20 minutes.

Classic Vanilla Dream

Making Time: 1.5 hours – 24 Cake Pops

Ingredients:
- *1 vanilla cake (homemade or store-bought)*
- *1 cup of vanilla frosting*
- *12 ounces of white chocolate (for coating)*
- *Sliced almonds for decoration*

Instructions:
- Crumble the vanilla cake into fine crumbs in a large bowl.
- Gradually add the vanilla frosting to the cake crumbs, starting with half a cup. Adjust the amount to achieve the desired consistency.
- Roll the mixture into uniform cake balls and insert cake pop sticks into each one.
- Melt the chocolate until runny and smooth, dipping the pops into it and allowing excess to drip off.
- Immediately decorate with sliced almonds while the coating is still wet. Place the cake pops on a drying rack.
- Allow the cake pops to set for about 15-20 minutes.

Luscious Lemon Poppy Seed Bliss

Making Time: 1.5 hours – 24 Cake Pops

Ingredients:
- *1 lemon poppy seed cake (homemade or store-bought)*
- *½ cup of lemon-flavored frosting*
- *12 ounces of white chocolate (for coating)*
- *Lemon zest and poppy seeds for decoration*

Instructions:
- Crumble the lemon poppy seed cake into fine crumbs in a large bowl.
- Gradually add the lemon-flavored frosting to the cake crumbs, starting with half a cup. Adjust the amount for the desired consistency.
- Roll the mixture into uniform balls and insert them with pop sticks.
- Melt the chocolate until runny and smooth, dipping the pops into it and allowing excess to drip off.
- While the coating is still wet, generously sprinkle lemon zest and poppy seeds on top of each cake pop for a burst of citrus and crunch.
- Allow the cake pops to set for about 15-20 minutes.

Oreo Cookie Crunch Pops

Making Time: 1.5 hours – 24 Cake Pops

Ingredients:
- *1 chocolate cake (homemade or store-bought)*
- *1 cup of cookies 'n cream-flavored frosting*
- *12 ounces of dark chocolate (for coating)*
- *Crushed Oreo cookies for decoration*

Instructions:
- Crumble the chocolate cake into fine crumbs in a large bowl.

- Gradually add the cookies 'n cream-flavored frosting to the cake crumbs, starting with half a cup. Adjust the amount for the desired consistency.
- Roll the mixture into uniform cake balls and insert cake pop sticks into each one.
- Melt the chocolate until runny and smooth, dipping the pops into it and allowing excess to drip off, then generously sprinkle crushed Oreo cookies on top of each cake pop.
- Allow the cake pops to set for about 15-20 minutes.

Raspberry Red Velvet Delight

Making Time: 1.5 hours – 24 Cake Pops

Ingredients:
- *1 red velvet cake (homemade or store-bought)*
- *½ cup of raspberry-flavored frosting*
- *12 ounces of white chocolate (for coating)*
- *Freeze-dried raspberries for garnish*

Instructions:
- Crumble the red velvet cake into fine crumbs in a large bowl.
- Gradually add the raspberry-flavored frosting to the cake crumbs, adjusting for the desired consistency.
- Roll the mixture into small balls and insert them with pop sticks.
- Melt the chocolate until runny and smooth, dipping the pops into it and allowing excess to drip off.
- While the coating is still wet, decorate with crushed freeze-dried raspberries. Set for 20 minutes before serving.

Rainbow Funfetti Carnival

Making Time: 1.5 hours – 24 Cake Pops

Ingredients:
- *1 funfetti cake (homemade or store-bought)*
- *½ cup of cream cheese frosting*
- *12 ounces of white chocolate (for coating)*
- *Rainbow nonpareils and edible glitter for decoration*

Instructions:
- Crumble the funfetti cake into fine crumbs in a large bowl.
- Gradually add the cream cheese frosting to the cake crumbs, adjusting the amount for the desired consistency.
- Roll the mixture into small balls and insert cake pop sticks into each one.
- Melt the chocolate until runny and smooth, dipping the pops into it and allowing excess to drip off.
- While the coating is still wet, generously decorate with rainbow nonpareils and a touch of edible glitter.
- Allow the cake pops to set for about 15-20 minutes.

Funfetti Extravaganza

Making Time: 1.5 hours – 24 Cake Pops

Ingredients:
- *1 funfetti cake (homemade or store-bought)*
- *1 cup of vanilla frosting*
- *12 ounces of white chocolate (for coating)*
- *Colorful sprinkles for decoration*

Instructions:
- Crumble the funfetti cake into fine crumbs in a large bowl.

- Gradually add the vanilla frosting to the cake crumbs, starting with half a cup. Adjust the amount for the desired consistency.
- Roll the mixture into uniform cake balls and insert cake pop sticks into each one.
- Melt the chocolate until runny and smooth, dipping the pops into it and allowing excess to drip off.
- Immediately decorate with colorful sprinkles.
- Allow the cake pops to set for about 15-20 minutes.

Double Chocolate Oreo Delight

Making Time: 1.5 hours – 24 Cake Pops

Ingredients:
- *1 chocolate cake (homemade or store-bought)*
- *1 cup of cookies 'n cream-flavored frosting*
- *12 ounces of white chocolate (for coating)*
- *Crushed Oreo cookies for decoration*

Instructions:
- Crumble the chocolate cake into fine crumbs in a large bowl.
- Gradually add the cookies 'n cream-flavored frosting to the cake crumbs, adjusting the amount for the desired consistency.
- Roll the mixture into uniform balls and insert cake pop sticks into each one.
- Melt the chocolate until smooth, dipping the pops into it, allowing excess to drip off. Place them on a drying rack.
- While the coating is still wet, generously sprinkle crushed Oreo cookies on top of each cake pop for a delightful crunch.
- Let them set for 20 minutes on a parchment paper.

Classic Strawberry Bliss

Making Time: 1.5 hours – 24 Cake Pops

Ingredients:
- *1 strawberry shortcake (homemade or store-bought)*
- *½ cup of strawberry-flavored frosting*
- *12 ounces of white chocolate (for coating)*
- *Fresh strawberry slices and crushed shortbread cookies for decoration*

Instructions:
- Crumble the strawberry shortcake into fine crumbs in a large bowl.
- Gradually add the strawberry-flavored frosting to the cake crumbs, starting with half a cup. Adjust the amount for the desired consistency.
- Roll the mixture into small balls and insert cake pop sticks into each one.
- Melt the chocolate until runny and smooth, dipping the pops into it and allowing excess to drip off. Place them on a drying rack.
- While the coating is still wet, decorate each cake pop with a slice of fresh strawberry and a sprinkle of crushed shortbread cookies. Allow to set for about 15-20 minutes.

Mocha Fudge Delight

Making Time: 1.5 hours – 24 Cake Pops

Ingredients:
- *1 chocolate fudge cake (homemade or store-bought)*
- *½ cup of chocolate frosting*
- *12 ounces of milk chocolate (for coating)*
- *Instant coffee granules for a subtle mocha flavor*
- *Crushed chocolate-covered espresso beans for decoration*

Instructions:

- Crumble the chocolate fudge cake into fine crumbs in a large bowl.
- Gradually add the chocolate frosting to the cake crumbs, adjusting the amount for the desired consistency.
- Sprinkle instant coffee granules to the mixture to introduce a subtle mocha flavor. Mix thoroughly.
- Roll the mixture into small balls and insert cake pop sticks into each one.
- Melt the chocolate until smooth, dipping the pops into it and allowing excess to drip off. While still wet, decorate each cake pop with crushed chocolate-covered espresso beans.
- Allow the cake pops to set for about 15-20 minutes.

Dark Chocolate Decadence

Making Time: 1.5 hours – 24 Cake Pops

Ingredients:

- *1 chocolate fudge cake (homemade or store-bought)*
- *1 cup of dark chocolate ganache (made with heavy cream and dark chocolate)*
- *Dark chocolate shavings or cocoa powder for decoration*

Instructions:

- Crumble the chocolate fudge cake into fine crumbs in a bowl.
- Gradually mix in the dark chocolate ganache until the cake crumbs are well coated. It should be fudgy and decadent.
- Roll the mixture into uniform cake balls and insert cake pop sticks into each one.
- Melt a bit of additional dark chocolate, dipping the pops into it. Allow any excess to drip off.
- Immediately after dipping, decorate the cake pops with dark chocolate shavings or a dusting of cocoa powder.
- Allow the cake pops to set for about 20-30 minutes.

Strawberry Lemonade Dream

Making Time: 1.5 hours – 24 Cake Pops

Ingredients:

- 1 strawberry lemonade cake (homemade or store-bought)
- ½ cup of lemon-flavored frosting
- 12 ounces of white chocolate (for coating)
- Lemon zest, fresh strawberry slices, and crushed shortbread cookies for decoration

Instructions:

- Crumble the strawberry lemonade cake into fine crumbs in a large bowl.
- Gradually add the lemon-flavored frosting to the cake crumbs, starting with half a cup. Adjust the amount for the desired consistency.
- Roll the mixture into uniform balls and insert cake pop sticks into each one.
- Melt the white chocolate and dip the pops into it, allowing excess to drip off. Place them on a drying rack.
- While the coating is still wet, decorate each cake pop with a sprinkle of lemon zest, a slice of fresh strawberry, and a touch of crushed shortbread cookies.
- Allow to set for about 15 or 20 minutes.

SEASONAL CAKE POPS

Easter Bunny Cake Pops

Making Time: 1.5 hours – 24 Cake Pops

Ingredients:

- *1 batch of prepared carrot cake crumbs (using carrot cake base)*
- *1 cup cream cheese frosting*
- *White candy melts*
- *Pink candy melts*
- *Mini marshmallows (for bunny tails)*
- *Pink sanding sugar (for bunny ears)*
- *Edible candy eyes*
- *Lollipop sticks*

Instructions:

- In a large bowl, combine the prepared carrot cake crumbs and cream cheese frosting. Mix until the mixture is well combined and can be easily shaped into cake balls.
- Shape the mixture into small cake balls, and insert lollipop sticks into each one. Place them on a baking sheet lined with parchment paper.
- Melt the white candy melts in a microwave-safe bowl, following the package instructions. Stir until smooth.
- Dip each cake pop into the melted white candy melts, allowing excess to drip off.
- While the white coating is still wet, attach a mini marshmallow to the back of the cake pop for the bunny's tail.
- Attach two edible candy eyes to the cake pop.
- Melt the pink candy melts in a microwave-safe bowl, following the package instructions. Stir until smooth.
- Dip the top of the cake pop into the pink candy melts to create bunny ears. Immediately sprinkle pink sanding sugar over the pink ears for a sparkly effect.
- Allow the cake pops to set and dry by placing them back on the parchment-lined baking sheet. Enjoy!

Love-Struck Valentine's Day Pops

Making Time: 1.5 hours – 24 Cake Pops

Ingredients:

- *1 batch of prepared red velvet cake base*
- *1 cup cream cheese frosting*
- *Red candy melts*
- *Valentine's Day-themed sprinkles (hearts, lips, Cupid's arrows, etc.)*
- *Lollipop sticks*

Instructions:

- In a large bowl, combine the prepared red velvet cake crumbs and the cream cheese frosting. Mix until the mixture is well combined and can be easily shaped into cake balls.
- Shape the mixture into small cake balls and insert lollipop sticks into each one. Place them on a baking sheet lined with parchment paper.
- Melt the red candy melts in a microwave-safe bowl, following the package instructions. Stir until smooth.
- Dip each cake pop into the melted red candy melts, allowing excess to drip off.
- While the candy coating is still wet, decorate the cake pops with Valentine's Day-themed sprinkles, adding a touch of love and sweetness.
- Allow the cake pops to set by placing them back on the parchment-lined baking sheet.
- Once they are completely dry, your Love-Struck Valentine's Day Pops are ready!

Christmas Tree Pops

Making Time: 1.5 hours – 24 Cake Pops

Ingredients:

- *1 batch of prepared chocolate cake crumbs (using chocolate cake)*
- *1 cup chocolate frosting*
- *Green candy melts*
- *Assorted colorful sprinkles and small candies for decoration*
- *Cake pop sticks*

Instructions:

- In a large bowl, combine the prepared chocolate cake crumbs and chocolate frosting. Mix until well combined.
- Shape the mixture into small cake balls and insert cake pop sticks into each one. Place them on a baking sheet lined with parchment paper.
- Melt the green candy melts in a microwave-safe bowl, following the package instructions. Stir until smooth.
- Dip each cake pop into the melted green candy melts, allowing excess to drip off.
- While the candy coating is still wet, decorate the cake pops with colorful sprinkles to resemble ornaments and small candies to mimic Christmas lights. You can also use mini-M&M's or small round candies.
- To create the tree trunk, you can use a small piece of a brownie or chocolate cake, shaped into a cone or cylinder, and attached to the bottom of the cake pop.
- Allow the cake pops to set by placing them back on the parchment-lined baking sheet.

Thanksgiving Pumpkin Spice Pops

Making Time: 1.5 hours – 24 Cake Pops

Ingredients:

- *1 batch of prepared pumpkin spice cake crumbs*
- *1 cup cream cheese frosting*
- *Orange candy melts*
- *Fall-themed sprinkles (e.g., leaves, pumpkins, or acorns)*
- *Cake pop sticks*

Instructions:

- In a large bowl, combine the prepared pumpkin spice cake crumbs and cream cheese frosting. Mix until well combined.
- Shape the mixture into small cake balls and insert cake pop sticks into each one. Place them on a baking sheet lined with parchment paper.
- Melt the orange candy melts in a microwave-safe bowl, following the package instructions. Stir until smooth.
- Dip each pumpkin spice cake pop into the melted orange candy melts, allowing excess to drip off.
- While the candy coating is still wet, decorate the cake pops with fall-themed sprinkles, embracing the colors and symbols of the season.
- Allow the cake pops to set by placing them back on the parchment-lined baking sheet.

Patriotic 4th of July Pops

Making Time: 1.5 hours – 24 Cake Pops

Ingredients:

- *1 batch of prepared vanilla cake crumbs (using vanilla cake base)*
- *1 cup white chocolate ganache (made white chocolate and cream)*
- *Red and blue candy melts*
- *Patriotic-themed sprinkles (stars, stripes, etc.)*
- *Lollipop sticks*

Instructions:

- In a large bowl, combine the prepared vanilla cake crumbs and the white chocolate ganache. Mix until the mixture is well combined and can be easily shaped into cake balls.
- Shape the mixture into small cake balls and insert lollipop sticks into each one. Place them on a baking sheet lined with parchment paper.
- Melt the red and blue candy melts in separate microwave-safe bowls, following the package instructions. Stir until smooth.
- Dip each cake pop into either the red or blue candy melts, allowing excess to drip off.
- While the candy coating is still wet, decorate the cake pops with patriotic-themed sprinkles, celebrating the colors of the 4th of July.
- Allow the cake pops to set by placing them back on the parchment-lined baking sheet.

Summertime Watermelon Cake Pops

Making Time: 2 hours – 24 Cake Pops

Ingredients:
- *1 batch of prepared watermelon-flavored cake crumbs*
- *1 cup green-tinted vanilla frosting*
- *1 cup pink-tinted vanilla frosting*
- *Mini chocolate chips (for watermelon seeds)*
- *Red and green candy melts*
- *Green and black food coloring (for watermelon rind)*
- *Lollipop sticks*

Instructions:
- In a large bowl, combine the prepared watermelon-flavored cake crumbs and the green-tinted vanilla frosting. Mix until the mixture is well combined and can be easily shaped into cake balls.

- Shape the mixture into small cake balls, and insert lollipop sticks into each one. Place them on a baking sheet lined with parchment paper.
- Melt the green candy melts and add a few drops of green food coloring to achieve the desired shade of green. Dip the cake pops into the green candy melts to create the watermelon rind. Allow excess to drip off.
- While the green coating is still wet, add mini chocolate chips to represent watermelon seeds. Place the cake pops back on the parchment-lined baking sheet to set.
- Melt the pink candy melts and dip the cake pops into the pink candy melts, covering the exposed cake ball. Allow excess to drip off.
- Before the pink coating sets, you can use black food coloring to paint thin lines on the pink surface to resemble the watermelon's stripes. Allow the cake pops to set and dry!

Fall Apple Cider Cake Pops

Making Time: 1.5 hours – 24 Cake Pops

Ingredients:
- *1 batch of prepared apple spice cake crumbs*
- *1 cup cream cheese frosting*
- *Caramel candy melts*
- *Crushed cinnamon graham crackers (for a coating)*
- *Small edible fall leaves (for decoration)*
- *Lollipop sticks*

Instructions:
- In a large bowl, combine the prepared apple spice cake crumbs and cream cheese frosting. Mix until the mixture is well combined and can be easily shaped into cake balls.

- Shape the mixture into small cake balls and insert lollipop sticks into each one. Place them on a baking sheet lined with parchment paper.
- Melt the caramel candy melts in a microwave-safe bowl, following the package instructions. Stir until smooth.
- Dip each cake pop into the melted caramel candy melts, allowing excess to drip off.
- Immediately roll the caramel-coated cake pop in crushed cinnamon graham crackers to give it a crunchy, apple cider flavor.
- Decorate the top of the cake pops with small edible fall leaves.
- Allow the cake pops to set by placing them back on the parchment-lined baking sheet.

Spooky Halloween Cake Pops

Making Time: 1.5 hours – 24 Cake Pops

Ingredients:
- *1 batch of prepared chocolate cake crumbs*
- *1 cup chocolate frosting*
- *Orange candy melts*
- *Black candy melts*
- *Candy eyes*
- *Halloween-themed sprinkles and decorations*
- *Cake pop sticks*

Instructions:
- In a large bowl, combine the prepared chocolate cake crumbs and chocolate frosting. Mix until well combined.
- Shape the mixture into small cake balls and insert cake pop sticks into each one. Place them on a baking sheet lined with parchment paper.

- Melt the orange candy melts and black candy melts in microwave-safe bowls, following the package instructions. Stir until smooth.
- Dip each cake pop into the melted orange candy melts, allowing excess to drip off. You can also drizzle some black candy melts to create a marbled effect.
- While the candy coating is still wet, decorate the cake pops with candy eyes and Halloween-themed sprinkles and decorations.
- Allow the cake pops to set by placing them back on the parchment-lined baking sheet.

DECADENT DESSERT-INSPIRED POPS

Caramel Apple Pie Pops

Making Time: 1.5 hours – 24 Cake Pops

Ingredients:

- 2 cups peeled, cored, and diced apples (e.g., Granny Smith)
- ½ cup granulated sugar
- ¼ cup unsalted butter
- ½ tsp ground cinnamon
- ¼ tsp ground nutmeg
- ¼ tsp salt
- 1 tbsp all-purpose flour
- 1 package refrigerated pie crusts (2 crusts)
- 1 egg, beaten
- ¼ cup caramel sauce
- Cake pop sticks

Instructions:

- Cook diced apples, granulated sugar, butter, cinnamon, nutmeg, and salt in a saucepan for about 15 minutes on medium heat. A tender but thick consistency is needed.
- Stir in the flour to thicken the filling. Remove from heat and let it cool.
- Roll out the refrigerated pic crusts and use a round cookie cutter to cut out small circles. Place a small spoonful of the cooled apple filling in the center of half of the pie crust circles.
- Brush the edges of the filled circles with beaten egg and place another pie crust circle on top. Press the edges together to seal the pops.
- Insert a cake pop stick into each pop and brush the tops with beaten egg.
- Bake in a preheated oven according to the pie crust package instructions or until the pops are golden brown.
- Drizzle caramel sauce over the pops while they are still warm. Dry completely and enjoy!

Cheesecake Dream Pops

Making Time: 1.5 hours – 24 Cake Pops

Ingredients:

- *8 ounces cream cheese, softened*
- *¼ cup confectioners' sugar*
- *1 tsp pure vanilla extract*
- *½ cup graham cracker crumbs*
- *½ cup fresh berries (e.g., strawberries, blueberries, or raspberries), chopped*
- *White chocolate chips, melted*
- *Cake pop sticks*

Instructions:

- Beat the softened cream cheese in a mixer until smooth.
- Add the confectioners' sugar and vanilla extract and continue to mix until well combined.
- Stir in the graham cracker crumbs and chopped fresh berries. The mixture should have a cheesecake-like consistency.
- Shape the mixture into small cheesecake pop-sized balls and place them on a baking sheet.
- Freeze for about 30 minutes or until firm.
- Insert cake pop sticks into the center of each pop and dip each pop into the melted white chocolate chips, allowing any excess to drip off.
- Place them back on parchment paper and let them set.

Tiramisu Truffle Pops

Making Time: 1.5 hours – 24 Cake Pops

Ingredients:

- *1 cup prepared espresso or strong coffee, cooled*
- *¼ cup coffee liqueur (e.g., Kahlúa)*
- *8 ounces mascarpone cheese*

- ¼ cup confectioners' sugar
- 1 tsp pure vanilla extract
- ½ cup ladyfingers, crushed into crumbs
- 1 cup semisweet or dark chocolate, melted
- Unsweetened cocoa powder (for dusting)
- Cake pop sticks

Instructions:

- Combine the espresso or coffee and coffee liqueur on a plate or a bowl. Set it aside.
- Mix the mascarpone cheese, confectioners' sugar, and vanilla extract until smooth in a mixer.
- Add the crushed ladyfingers to the mascarpone and stir until well combined.
- Shape the mixture into small balls and place them on a baking sheet, then freeze the batch for about 30 minutes until firm.
- Insert cake pop sticks into the center of each ball, then dip them into the melted chocolate.
- Before the chocolate sets, dust the truffle pops with unsweetened cocoa powder for the classic Tiramisu flavor.
- Allow them to set on parchment paper.

Pina Colada Paradise Pops

Making Time: 1.5 hours – 24 Cake Pops

Ingredients:

- 1 cup crushed pineapple, drained
- ½ cup sweetened shredded coconut
- ¼ cup white rum (optional)
- ¼ cup cream of coconut
- 1 cup confectioners' sugar
- 1 package vanilla wafer cookies, crushed
- White candy melts
- Shredded coconut (for decoration)

- *Maraschino cherries (for decoration)*
- *Cake pop sticks*

Instructions:

- Combine the crushed pineapple, sweetened shredded coconut, white rum (if using), and cream of coconut. Mix well and stir in the confectioners' sugar for thickness.
- Shape the mixture into small balls and place them on a baking sheet. Freeze for about 30 minutes or until firm.
- Insert cake pop sticks into the center of each pop.
- Melt the white candy melts in a microwave-safe bowl following the package instructions. Stir until smooth.
- Dip each pop into the melted white candy melts, allowing any excess to drip off, then sprinkle shredded coconut on the pops for a tropical touch.
- Top each pop with a maraschino cherry.

Key Lime Pie Pops

Making Time: 1.5 hours – 24 Cake Pops

Ingredients:

- *1 cup graham cracker crumbs*
- *2 tbsp granulated sugar*
- *¼ cup unsalted butter, melted*
- *1 can (14 ounces) sweetened condensed milk*
- *½ cup key lime juice (regular lime juice can be used)*
- *Zest of 2 limes*
- *Green candy melts*
- *Cake pop sticks*

Instructions:

- Add cracker crumbs, sugar, and melted butter to a bowl and stir to combine. Mix until the mixture resembles wet sand.
- Press the graham cracker mixture into small balls and place them on a baking sheet, then insert with the pop sticks.

- Combine the condensed milk, lime juice, and zest until well combined, to make the dipping.
- Dip each cracker ball into the green candy melts, allowing any excess to drip off. Set and serve.

Bananas Foster Bliss Bites

Making Time: 1.5 hours – 24 Cake Pops

Ingredients:
- *2 ripe bananas, mashed*
- *½ cup crushed graham crackers*
- *¼ cup brown sugar*
- *2 tbsp dark rum*
- *1 tsp ground cinnamon*
- *½ cup chopped pecans (optional)*
- *White chocolate chips, melted*
- *Cake pop sticks*

Instructions:
- Wish together mashed bananas, crushed graham crackers, brown sugar, dark rum, ground cinnamon, and chopped pecans (if using) with a fork or a spoon until well combined.
- Shape the mixture into small bite-sized balls and place them on a baking sheet. Freeze for about 30 minutes or until firm.
- Insert cake pop sticks into the center of each ball and dip them in the melted white chocolate chips.
- Allow them to set on parchment paper before serving.

Churro-Chocolate Fusion Pops

Making Time: 2 hours – 24 Cake Pops

Ingredients:

70

- *1 batch of chocolate cake base*
- *Chocolate frosting base*
- *½ cup granulated sugar*
- *1 tsp ground cinnamon*
- *White chocolate chips, melted*
- *Cake pop sticks*

Instructions:

- Prepare a batch of chocolate cake pops using your favorite chocolate cake recipe and chocolate frosting.
- Combine the granulated sugar and ground cinnamon in a shallow bowl or plate.
- Dip each chocolate cake pop into the melted white chocolate chips, allowing any excess to drip off.
- Immediately roll the cake pop in the cinnamon-sugar mixture to create a churro-like coating. Set and serve!

Chocolate Peanut Butter Cup Pops

Making Time: 1.5 hours – 24 Cake Pops

Ingredients:

- *1 cup creamy peanut butter*
- *½ cup confectioners' sugar*
- *1 cup crushed chocolate sandwich cookies (e.g., Oreo)*
- *1 cup milk chocolate chips, melted*
- *Cake pop sticks*

Instructions:

- Combine the creamy peanut butter, confectioners' sugar, and crushed chocolate sandwich cookies in a bowl.
- Shape the mixture into small balls and place them on a baking sheet and insert them with pop sticks.
- Dip each ball into the melted milk chocolate chips, allowing any excess to drip off. Set and serve.

Cookies and Cream Delight Pops

Making Time: 2 hours – 24 Cake Pops

Ingredients:
- *1 batch of chocolate cake (made using your favorite chocolate cake recipe)*
- *Chocolate frosting of choice*
- *1 cup crushed chocolate sandwich cookies (e.g., Oreo)*
- *White chocolate chips, melted*
- *Cake pop sticks*

Instructions:
- Prepare a batch of chocolate cake pops using your favorite chocolate cake recipe.
- Combine the crushed chocolate sandwich cookies with the chocolate cake crumbs.
- Shape the mixture into small balls and place them on a baking sheet, then insert with the pop sticks.
- Dip each pop into the melted white chocolate chips, allowing any excess to drip off. Set and serve.

Raspberry Chocolate Truffle Pops

Making Time: 2 hours – 24 Cake Pops

Ingredients:
- *1 batch of chocolate cake pops (made using your favorite chocolate cake recipe)*
- *Chocolate frosting of choice*
- *½ cup seedless raspberry jam*
- *Dark chocolate chips, melted*
- *Freeze-dried raspberries (for decoration)*
- *Cake pop sticks*

Instructions:

- Prepare a batch of chocolate cake pops using your favorite chocolate cake and frosting recipe.
- Stir the seedless raspberry jam to loosen it slightly.
- Shape the chocolate cake pop mixture into small balls and make a small well in the center of each ball.
- Fill the well with a small amount of jam, then seal it by reshaping the ball. Carefully insert pop sticks.
- Dip each pop into the melted dark chocolate chips, allowing any excess to drip off, then decorate the pops with crushed freeze-dried raspberries for a burst of color and flavor.
- Allow them to set on parchment paper.

SPECIALTY & GOURMET POPS

Lavender Honey Elegance Pops

Making Time: 2 hours – 24 Cake Pops

Ingredients:
- *1 batch of vanilla cake (using vanilla cake base)*
- *Vanilla frosting*
- *¼ cup lavender honey*
- *White chocolate chips, melted*
- *Dried lavender buds (for decoration)*
- *Cake pop sticks*

Instructions:
- Prepare a batch of vanilla cake pops using your favorite vanilla cake and frosting recipe.
- In a small bowl, warm the lavender honey to make it more fluid.
- Shape the vanilla cake pop mixture into small balls, making a small well in the center of each ball.
- Fill the well with a small amount of lavender honey, then seal it by reshaping the ball.
- Insert cake pop sticks into the center of each pop and dip them into the melted white chocolate chips.
- Before the coating sets, sprinkle dried lavender buds on top for decoration, wait for them to set and serve.

Black Forest Gateau Pops

Making Time: 2 hours – 24 Cake Pops

Ingredients:
- *1 batch of chocolate cake (using chocolate cake base)*
- *Chocolate frosting*
- *¼ cup cherry jam or preserves*
- *¼ cup kirsch (cherry brandy) or cherry juice*

- *Dark chocolate chips, melted*
- *Maraschino cherries (for decoration)*
- *Cake pop sticks*

Instructions:

- Prepare a batch of chocolate cake pops using your favorite chocolate cake and frosting recipe.
- In a small bowl, mix the cherry jam with kirsch (or cherry juice) to create a cherry filling.
- Shape the chocolate cake pop mixture into small balls, making a small well in the center of each ball.
- Fill the well with a small amount of cherry filling, then seal it by reshaping the ball.
- Insert cake pop sticks into the center of each pop and dip them into the melted dark chocolate chips, allowing any excess to drip off.
- Before the coating sets, top each pop with a maraschino cherry for decoration. Set and serve!

Espresso Martini Mocha Pops

Making Time: 2 hours – 24 Cake Pops

Ingredients:

- *1 batch of chocolate cake*
- *¼ cup brewed espresso or strong coffee, cooled*
- *¼ cup coffee liqueur (e.g., Kahlúa)*
- *Dark chocolate chips, melted*
- *Coffee beans (for decoration)*
- *Cake pop sticks*

Instructions:

- Prepare a batch of chocolate cake using your favorite chocolate cake recipe.
- In a mixing bowl, combine the brewed espresso or strong coffee with the coffee liqueur. Add cake crumbs and mix.

- Shape the chocolate cake pop mixture into small truffle-sized balls and place them on a baking sheet.
- Insert cake pop sticks into the center of each pop.
- Dip each pop into the melted dark chocolate chips, allowing any excess to drip off, then top each pop with a coffee bean for decoration. Set and enjoy!

Champagne Celebration Pops

Making Time: 2 hours – 24 Cake Pops

Ingredients:
- *1 batch of vanilla cake*
- *¼ cup champagne or sparkling wine*
- *White chocolate chips, melted*
- *Edible gold leaf or gold luster dust (for decoration)*
- *Cake pop sticks*

Instructions:
- Prepare a batch of vanilla cake pops using your favorite vanilla cake recipe.
- In a small bowl, mix the champagne or sparkling wine with the vanilla cake crumbs.
- Shape the mixture into small balls and place them on a baking sheet, then insert them with cake pop sticks.
- Dip each pop into the melted white chocolate chips.
- Drip off the excess and decorate with edible gold leaf or a sprinkle of gold luster dust for a touch of elegance.

Truffle-Infused Wine Pops

Making Time: 2 hours – 24 Cake Pops

Ingredients:

- 1 batch of chocolate cake
- ¼ cup red wine (choose your favorite)
- Dark chocolate chips, melted
- Edible gold leaf or gold luster dust (for decoration)
- Cake pop sticks

Instructions:

- Prepare a batch of chocolate cake pops using your favorite chocolate cake recipe.
- In a small bowl, mix the red wine with the chocolate cake crumbs to create a wine-infused cake mixture.
- Shape the mixture into small wine balls and place them on a baking sheet.
- Insert cake pop sticks into the center of each pop and dip them into the melted dark chocolate chips, allowing any excess to drip off.
- Before the coating sets, decorate with edible gold leaf or a sprinkle of gold luster dust for an elegant touch. Set and serve!

White Chocolate Strawberry Truffle Pops

Making Time: 2 hours – 24 Cake Pops

Ingredients:

- 1 batch of vanilla cake pops (made using your favorite vanilla cake and frosting recipe)
- ¼ cup strawberry preserves or fresh strawberries
- White chocolate chips, melted
- Freeze-dried strawberries (for decoration)
- Cake pop sticks

Instructions:

- Prepare a batch of vanilla cake pops using your favorite vanilla cake and frosting recipe.

- Mix the strawberry preserves or fresh strawberries to create a fruity filling.
- Shape the vanilla cake pop mixture into small balls, making a small well in the center of each ball. Fill the well with a small amount of strawberry filling and seal it by reshaping the ball.
- Insert cake pop sticks into the center of each pop.
- Dip each pop into the melted white chocolate chips, allowing any excess to drip off. Decorate with crushed freeze-dried strawberries for a burst of color and flavor.
- Allow them to set on parchment paper.

Earl Grey Tea Infusion Pops

Making Time: 2 hours – 24 Cake Pops

Ingredients:
- *1 batch of vanilla cake pops*
- *¼ cup Earl Grey tea, brewed and cooled*
- *White chocolate chips, melted*
- *Dried lavender buds (for decoration)*
- *Cake pop sticks*

Instructions:
- Prepare a batch of vanilla cake pops using your favorite vanilla cake recipe.
- Mix together the brewed and cooled Earl Grey tea with the vanilla cake crumbs.
- Shape the mixture into small balls and place them on a baking sheet, inserting them with pop sticks.
- Dip each pop into the melted white chocolate chips, allowing any excess to drip off.
- Before the coating sets, decorate with dried lavender buds for a delightful touch. Allow them to set on parchment paper.

Saffron Pistachio Delights

Making Time: 2 hours – 24 Cake Pops

Ingredients:
- *1 batch of vanilla cake pops*
- *A pinch of saffron threads, steeped in 1 tbsp of warm milk*
- *½ cup shelled pistachios, finely ground*
- *White chocolate chips, melted*
- *Crushed pistachios (for decoration)*
- *Cake pop sticks*

Instructions:
- Prepare a batch of vanilla cake pops using your favorite vanilla cake recipe.
- Steep a pinch of saffron threads in warm milk, allowing it to infuse, then combine the milk with the vanilla cake crumbs.
- Shape the mixture into small balls and place them on a baking sheet.
- Insert cake pop sticks into the center of each pop and dip them into the melted white chocolate chips.
- Drip off the excess and sprinkle crushed pistachios on top for a delightful touch, before the coating sets.
- Allow them to set on parchment paper.

VEGAN CAKE POPS

Vegan Lemon Blueberry Delight Pops

Making Time: 2 hours – 24 Cake Pops

Ingredients:
- *1 batch of vegan lemon cake base*
- *¼ cup vegan lemon curd (store-bought or homemade)*
- *Blueberry glaze (made with ¼ cup blueberry puree, 1 cup powdered sugar and 1 tsp lemon juice)*
- *Fresh blueberries (for decoration)*
- *Cake pop sticks*

Instructions:
- Prepare a batch of vegan lemon cake pops using a vegan lemon cake recipe. Mix in the lemon curd.
- Shape the lemon cake pop mixture into small balls and place them on a baking sheet. Insert cake pop sticks into the center of each pop.
- Prepare the blueberry glaze by mixing all the glaze ingredients together. If it is too thin, add more sugar, it is too thick, and add more puree. Adjust the sweetest to taste.
- Dip each pop into the blueberry glaze, then, top each pop with a fresh blueberry for decoration. Set and enjoy!

Vegan Chocolate Peanut Butter Pops

Making Time: 2 hours – 24 Cake Pops

Ingredients:
- *1 batch of vegan chocolate cake base*
- *½ cup peanut butter (check for dairy-free)*
- *Vegan chocolate chips, melted*
- *Crushed peanuts (for decoration)*
- *Cake pop sticks*

Instructions:

- Prepare a batch of vegan chocolate cake pops using a vegan chocolate cake recipe. In a small bowl, warm the peanut butter and add it to the cake mixture. Stir to combine.
- Shape the chocolate cake pop mixture into small balls and place them on a baking sheet. Insert with pop sticks.
- Dip each pop into the melted vegan chocolate chips, allowing any excess to drip off.
- Before the coating sets, sprinkle crushed peanuts on top for a delightful crunch, then let them set for a few minutes.

Vegan Vanilla Cake Recipe

Making Time: 40 min – 24 Cake Pops

Ingredients:
- 1 ½ cups flour (all-purpose works best)
- 1 cup white or brown sugar
- 1 tsp baking soda
- A pinch of salt
- 1 cup almond milk (or any plant-based milk of your choice)
- ⅓ cup vegetable oil (or melted coconut oil)
- 1 tbsp white or apple cider vinegar
- 1 tsp vanilla extract

Instructions:
- Preheat your oven to 350°F (175°C). Grease and flour an 8-inch round cake pan.
- Separately whisk together solid and wet ingredients in separate bowls or plates.
- Once well combined, mix them together, pouring wet mixture into the dry ingredients. Do not overmix, a few lumps are not the problem.
- Pour the cake batter into the greased 9-inch round cake pan.
- Transfer to the oven and bake on 350°F (175°C) for about 25-30 minutes.

- After the cake cools a little bit, it is ready to use in your Vegan Cake Pops recipes!
- *Note: This is a basic vanilla cake recipe, but you can customize it by adding flavorings like cocoa powder for chocolate cake, or lemon zest for lemon cake. You can adjust the sweetness to your preference by adding more or less sugar.*

Vegan Caramel Apple Pie Pops

Making Time: 2 hours – 24 Cake Pops

Ingredients:
- *1 batch of vegan apple cake base*
- *Vegan caramel sauce (store-bought or homemade)*
- *Vegan white chocolate chips (for drizzling)*
- *Crushed walnuts (for decoration)*
- *Cake pop sticks*

Instructions:
- Prepare a batch of vegan apple cake pops using a vegan apple cake recipe.
- Warm the vegan caramel sauce to make it spreadable. Add it to the crumbs.
- Shape the apple cake pop mixture into small balls and place them on a baking sheet. Insert them with pop sticks.
- Dip each pop into the melted vegan white chocolate chips, allowing any excess to drip off, then sprinkle with crushed walnuts for a delightful crunch.
- Finally, drizzle with warmed vegan caramel sauce.

Vegan Red Velvet Bliss Pops

Making Time: 2 hours – 24 Cake Pops

Ingredients:
- *1 batch of vegan red velvet cake*
- *Vegan cream cheese frosting (store-bought or homemade)*
- *Vegan red candy melts*
- *Vegan white chocolate chips (for decoration)*
- *Cake pop sticks*

Instructions:
- Prepare a batch of vegan red velvet cake pops using a vegan red velvet cake recipe. Combine the vegan cream cheese frosting with the cake crumbs in a bowl.
- Shape the mixture into small balls and place them on a baking sheet. Insert cake pop sticks into the center of each pop.
- Dip each pop into the melted red candy melts, allowing any excess to drip off.
- Drizzle with melted vegan white chocolate for decoration and allow them to set on parchment paper.
- *Note: vegan cream frosting is made similarly to the regular (non-vegan) frosting, you just have to replace animal-based ingredients with plant-based ones.*

Vegan Chocolate Coconut Paradise Pops

Making Time: 2 hours – 24 Cake Pops

Ingredients:
- *1 batch of vegan chocolate cake base*
- *Vegan chocolate ganache*
- *Shredded coconut (for decoration)*
- *Cake pop sticks*

Instructions:

- Prepare a batch of vegan chocolate cake using a vegan chocolate cake recipe.
- Create a vegan chocolate ganache using coconut milk and cream instead of regular dairy milk or cream. Mix with the crumbs.
- Shape the chocolate cake pop mixture into small chocolate coconut-sized balls and place them on a baking sheet.
- Insert cake pop sticks into the center of each pop.
- Dip each pop into the vegan chocolate ganache, allowing any excess to drip off, then roll the pop in shredded.
- Allow them to set on parchment paper.

INTERNATIONAL POPS

Italian Cannoli Cake Pops

Making Time: 2 hours – 24 Cake Pops

Ingredients:
- *1 batch of Italian cannoli cake base*
- *Cannoli cream filling (store-bought or homemade)*
- *Dark chocolate chips, melted*
- *Chopped pistachios (for decoration)*
- *Cake pop sticks*

Instructions:
- Prepare a batch of Italian cannoli cake using an Italian cannoli cake recipe.
- Mix the cannoli cream filling in a bowl to make it more spreadable and add it to the cannoli cake.
- Shape the cannoli mixture into small balls and place them on a baking sheet. Insert with a cake pop stick.
- Dip each pop into the melted dark chocolate chips, allowing any excess to drip off. Before the coating sets, sprinkle chopped pistachios.

Matcha Green Tea Zen Pops

Making Time: 2 hours – 24 Cake Pops

Ingredients:
- *1 batch of matcha green tea cake base*
- *Matcha green tea frosting (store-bought or homemade)*
- *White chocolate chips, melted*
- *Matcha green tea powder (for decoration)*
- *Cake pop sticks*

Instructions:
- Prepare a batch of matcha green tea cake base using a matcha green tea cake recipe.

- Combine the matcha cake crumbs with matcha green tea frosting in a bowl. Shape the mixture into small balls and place them on a baking sheet.
- Insert cake pop sticks into the center of each pop, then dip them into the melted white chocolate chips.
- Before the coating sets, dust with matcha green tea powder.

Greek Baklava Bites

Making Time: 2 hours – 24 Cake Pops

Ingredients:
- *1 batch of baklava-flavored cake base*
- *Vanilla frosting*
- *Honey syrup*
- *Chopped pistachios and walnuts (for decoration)*
- *Cake pop sticks*

Instructions:
- Prepare a batch of baklava-flavored cake pops using a baklava-flavored cake recipe and vanilla frosting.
- Shape the cake pop mixture into small balls and place them on a baking sheet, then insert them with cake pop sticks.
- In a saucepan, prepare the honey syrup by combining equal parts honey, sugar, and water. Bring to a simmer and let it thicken slightly. Allow it to cool.
- Drizzle the honey syrup over each pop, allowing it to soak in and add that characteristic baklava sweetness.
- Before the syrup sets, sprinkle with chopped pistachios and walnuts for a nutty and crunchy topping. Set and enjoy!

Mochi Madness Pops

Making Time: 1.5 hours – 24 Cake Pops

Ingredients:
- *1 batch of mochi-flavored cake base and milk frosting*
- *Sweetened condensed milk or coconut milk (for dipping)*
- *Sweet rice flour (for dusting)*
- *Cake pop sticks*

Instructions:
- Prepare a batch of mochi-flavored cake pops using a mochi-flavored cake recipe and frosting. Shape the mixture into small balls and place them on a baking sheet.
- Insert cake pop sticks into the center of each pop.
- Dip the pops into sweetened condensed milk or coconut milk, then dust with sweet rice flour for that traditional mochi appearance. Allow to set on parchment paper.

French Macaron-Inspired Pops

Making Time: 2 hours – 24 Cake Pops

Ingredients:
- *1 batch of macaron-flavored cake*
- *Macaron-flavored buttercream (store-bought or homemade)*
- *Pastel-colored candy melts (for coating)*
- *Edible pearl decorations (for decoration)*
- *Cake pop sticks*

Instructions:
- Prepare a batch of macaron-flavored cake base using a macaron-flavored cake recipe. Add macaron-flavored buttercream with the cake crumbs and combine well.
- Shape the mixture into small balls and place them on a baking sheet, then insert them with cake pop sticks.

- Melt pastel-colored candy melts following the package instructions. Dip each pop into the candy melts, allowing any excess to drip off.
- Decorate with edible pearl decorations for that elegant macaron look. Allow them to set on parchment paper.

Indian Gulab Jamun Pops

Making Time: 2 hours – 24 Cake Pops

Ingredients:
- *1 batch of gulab jamun-flavored cake base*
- *Rose-flavored syrup (store-bought or homemade)*
- *Chopped pistachios and edible rose petals (for decoration)*
- *Cake pop sticks*

Instructions:
- Prepare a batch of gulab jamun-flavored cake pops using a gulab jamun-flavored cake and frosting recipe.
- Shape the gulab cake pop mixture into small balls and place them on a baking sheet. Insert with cake pop sticks.
- Warm the rose-flavored syrup in a pan. You can make it by infusing rose water or rose essence into a simple syrup.
- Dip each pop into the warm rose syrup, allowing it to soak in and infuse the cake with the rose flavor.
- Before the syrup sets, decorate with chopped pistachios and edible rose petals. Serve and enjoy once set!

Mexican Churro Dulce Pops

Making Time: 2 hours – 24 Cake Pops

Ingredients:
- *1 batch of Mexican churro cake base and chocolate frosting*

- *Dulce de leche or caramel sauce (store-bought or homemade)*
- *Cinnamon-sugar coating*
- *Cake pop sticks*

Instructions:

- Prepare a batch of Mexican churro cake pops using a Mexican churro cake and chocolate frosting recipe. Shape into small balls and place them on a baking sheet.
- Insert with pop sticks, then roll each pop in a bowl of cinnamon-sugar coating until well coated.
- Drizzle with dulce de leche or caramel sauce for sweetness.
- Allow them to set on parchment paper.

Japanese Sakura Cherry Blossom Pops

Making Time: 2 hours – 24 Cake Pops

Ingredients:

- *1 batch of cherry blossom-flavored cake and frosting*
- *Sakura cherry blossom syrup (store-bought or homemade)*
- *Edible cherry blossom petals (for decoration)*
- *Cake pop sticks*

Instructions:

- Prepare a batch of cherry blossom-flavored cake using a cherry blossom-flavored cake and frosting recipe.
- Shape the cherry cake pop mixture into small balls and place them on a baking sheet, then insert with sticks.
- Warm the sakura cherry blossom syrup in a pan. You can make it by infusing cherry blossom essence or syrup into a simple syrup.
- Dip each pop into the warm syrup, allowing it to absorb the delicate cherry blossom flavor.
- Before the syrup sets, decorate with edible cherry blossom petals for a visually stunning and aromatic touch.

HEALTHY & DIETARY-FRIENDLY POPS

Gluten-Free Red Velvet Pops

Making Time: 2 hours – 24 Cake Pops

Ingredients:
- *1 batch of gluten-free red velvet cake base*
- *Greek yogurt or dairy-free yogurt (for frosting)*
- *Gluten-free red velvet cake crumbs (for decoration)*
- *Fresh raspberries (for topping)*
- *Cake pop sticks*

Instructions:
- Prepare a batch of gluten-free red velvet cake base using a gluten-free red velvet cake recipe. Mix Greek yogurt or dairy-free yogurt with the cake crumbs.
- Shape the mixture into small red balls and place them on a baking sheet, then insert them with cake pop sticks.
- Coat each pop with the yogurt frosting. Before the frosting sets, roll in gluten-free red velvet cake crumbs.
- Top each pop with a fresh raspberry for a burst of fruity goodness.

Nut-Free Sunflower Seed Pops

Making Time: 2 hours – 24 Cake Pops

Ingredients:
- *1 batch of nut-free sunflower seed cake base*
- *Sunflower seed butter (for frosting)*
- *Shredded coconut or sunflower seeds (for decoration)*
- *Cake pop sticks*

Instructions:
- Prepare a batch of nut-free sunflower seed cake pops using a nut-free sunflower seed cake recipe. Mix sunflower seed butter with the cake crumbs.

- Shape the mixture into small balls and place them on a baking sheet, then insert them with cake pop sticks.
- Coat each pop with the sunflower seed butter frosting. Before the frosting sets, roll in shredded coconut or sunflower seeds.

Sugar-Free Berry Bliss Bites

Making Time: 2 hours – 24 Cake Pops

Ingredients:
- *1 batch of sugar-free berry-flavored cake base*
- *Sugar-free Greek yogurt or dairy-free yogurt (for frosting)*
- *Fresh mixed berries (blueberries, strawberries, raspberries) for decoration*
- *Cake pop sticks*

Instructions:
- Prepare a batch of sugar-free berry-flavored cake base using a sugar-free berry cake recipe. Mix sugar-free Greek yogurt or dairy-free yogurt with the cake crumbs.
- Shape the mixture into small balls and place them on a baking sheet, then insert them with cake pop sticks.
- Coat each pop with the yogurt frosting. Before it sets, decorate with fresh mixed berries like blueberries, strawberries, and raspberries.

Paleo Pineapple Upside-Down Pops

Making Time: 2 hours – 24 Cake Pops

Ingredients:
- *1 batch of paleo pineapple upside-down cake base*
- *Honey or maple syrup (for drizzling)*
- *Dried pineapple rings or chunks (for decoration)*

- *Cake pop sticks*

Instructions:
- Prepare a batch of paleo pineapple upside-down cake base using a paleo pineapple upside-down cake recipe.
- Shape the mixture into small balls and place them on a baking sheet, then insert them with cake pop sticks.
- Drizzle with honey or maple syrup for natural sweetness and decorate with dried pineapple rings or chunks. Set and serve!

Keto-Friendly Peanut Butter Pops

Making Time: 2 hours – 24 Cake Pops

Ingredients:
- *1 batch of keto-friendly peanut butter cake base*
- *Sugar-free peanut butter or almond butter (for frosting)*
- *Crushed sugar-free chocolate or dark chocolate (for decoration)*
- *Cake pop sticks*

Instructions:
- Prepare a batch of keto-friendly peanut butter cake base using a keto-friendly peanut butter cake recipe. Mix sugar-free peanut butter or almond butter with the cake crumbs.
- Shape the mixture into small balls and place them on a baking sheet, then insert them with cake pop sticks.
- Coat each pop with sugar-free peanut butter or almond butter frosting.
- Before it sets, sprinkle with crushed sugar-free chocolate or dark chocolate for a keto-friendly touch.

Dairy-Free Coconut Almond Pops

Making Time: 2 hours – 24 Cake Pops

Ingredients:

- *1 batch of dairy-free coconut almond cake base*
- *Dairy-free coconut cream (for frosting)*
- *Shredded coconut and sliced almonds (for decoration)*
- *Cake pop sticks*

Instructions:

- Prepare a batch of dairy-free coconut almond cake base using a dairy-free coconut almond cake recipe. Mix dairy-free coconut cream with the cake crumbs.
- Shape the mixture into small balls and place them on a baking sheet, then insert them with cake pop sticks.
- Coat each pop with the coconut cream frosting and roll in a mixture of coconut and almonds for a delightful crunch. Set and serve.

Low-Carb Minty Fresh Pops

Making Time: 2 hours – 24 Cake Pops

Ingredients:

- *1 batch of low-carb mint-flavored cake base*
- *Sugar-free mint frosting (store-bought or homemade)*
- *Sugar-free chocolate chips or cacao nibs (for decoration)*
- *Cake pop sticks*

Instructions:

- Prepare a batch of low-carb mint-flavored cake base using a low-carb mint cake recipe. Combine with the mint frosting.
- Shape the mixture into small balls and place them on a baking sheet, then insert them with cake pop sticks.

- Coat each pop with mint frosting and decorate with chocolate chips or cacao nibs. Allow them to set on parchment paper.

KIDS & FUN POPS

Rainbow Unicorn Magic Pops

Making Time: 2 hours – 24 Cake Pops

Ingredients:

- *1 batch of vanilla cake base*
- *Vanilla frosting*
- *Rainbow-colored candy melts (red, orange, yellow, green, blue, and purple)*
- *Edible gold stars and rainbow sprinkles (for decoration)*
- *Cake pop sticks*

Instructions:

- Prepare a batch of vanilla cake using a vanilla cake recipe. Mix the vanilla frosting with the cake crumbs to create a smooth and pliable mixture.
- Shape the mixture into small balls and place them on a baking sheet. Insert cake pop sticks into the center of each pop.
- Melt each color of the rainbow-colored candy melts separately according to the package instructions.
- Dip each pop into the melted candy melts, creating a rainbow pattern by dipping in different colors. Allow any excess to drip off.
- While the coating is still wet, decorate with edible gold stars and rainbow sprinkles. Allow them to set, then serve.

Space Adventure Rocket Pops

Making Time: 2 hours – 24 Cake Pops

Ingredients:

- *1 batch of chocolate cake base*
- *Chocolate frosting*
- *Silver-colored candy melts (for coating)*
- *Small colorful candy-coated chocolates (for rocket accents)*

- *Cake pop sticks*

Instructions:
- Prepare a batch of chocolate cake using a chocolate cake recipe. Mix the chocolate frosting with the cake crumbs.
- Shape the mixture into small rocket-sized balls and place them on a baking sheet. Insert cake pop sticks into the center of each pop.
- Melt the silver-colored candy melts according to the package instructions.
- Dip each pop into the melted silver candy melts, allowing any excess to drip off, then attach small colorful candy-coated chocolates as rocket accents to create a rocket shape.
- Allow them to set on parchment paper.

Dinosaur Egg Cake Pops

Making Time: 2 hours – 24 Cake Pops

Ingredients:
- *1 batch of green-colored cake base*
- *Chocolate or vanilla frosting*
- *Speckled candy melts (for coating)*
- *Edible dinosaur decorations (small plastic or edible toppers)*
- *Cake pop sticks*

Instructions:
- Prepare a batch of green-colored cake using a green-colored cake recipe.
- Mix the chocolate or vanilla frosting with the cake crumbs to create a smooth and pliable mixture.
- Shape the mixture into small dinosaur egg-sized balls and place them on a baking sheet. Insert the balls with pop sticks.
- Melt the speckled candy melts according to the package instructions.

- Dip each pop into the melted speckled candy melts, creating a speckled appearance reminiscent of dinosaur eggs. Allow any excess to drip off.
- While the coating is still wet, add edible dinosaur decorations as toppers.

Cookie Monster's Cookie Pops

Making Time: 2 hours – 24 Cake Pops

Ingredients:
- *1 batch of chocolate chip cookie cake base*
- *Cookie frosting (vanilla frosting with blue coloring)*
- *Edible candy eyes*
- *Mini chocolate chip cookies (for decoration)*
- *Cake pop sticks*

Instructions:
- Prepare a batch of chocolate chip cookie cake using a chocolate chip cookie cake recipe. Mix the blue cookie frosting with the cake crumbs.
- Shape the mixture into small cookie-sized balls and place them on a baking sheet. Insert with pop sticks.
- Use cookie frosting to coat each pop, creating Cookie Monster's blue fur. While the frosting is still wet, add edible candy eyes for Cookie Monster's eyes. Decorate with mini chocolate chip cookies, allow to set, and serve.

Princess Castle Pops

Making Time: 2 hours – 24 Cake Pops

Ingredients:
- *1 batch of pink or pastel-colored cake base*
- *Vanilla frosting*
- *Pastel-colored candy melts (for coating)*
- *Edible pearl decorations and edible princess figurine toppers (for decoration)*
- *Cake pop sticks*

Instructions:
- Prepare a batch of pink or pastel-colored cake using a princess-themed vanilla cake recipe. Mix the vanilla frosting with the cake crumbs.
- Shape the mixture into small castle-sized balls and place them on a baking sheet. Insert them with pop sticks.
- Melt the pastel-colored candy melts according to the package instructions.
- Dip each pop into the melted candy melts, allowing any excess to drip off.
- While the coating is wet, decorate with edible pearl decorations and add edible princess figurine toppers.

Under the Sea Mermaid Pops

Making Time: 2 hours – 24 Cake Pops

Ingredients:
- *1 batch of aqua or ocean-colored cake base*
- *Blue or aqua frosting*
- *Mermaid tail and seashell decorations (store-bought or homemade)*
- *Edible glitter (for decoration)*
- *Cake pop sticks*

Instructions:

- Prepare a batch of aqua or ocean-colored cake using a sea-themed cake recipe. Mix the blue or aqua frosting with the cake crumbs.
- Shape the mixture into small mermaid tail-sized balls and place them on a baking sheet. Insert with the cake pop sticks.
- Dip each pop into the blue or aqua frosting, then decorate with mermaid tail and seashell decorations.
- Sprinkle with edible glitter for that magical underwater effect.

Superhero Power Burst Pops

Making Time: 2 hours – 24 Cake Pops

Ingredients:

- *1 batch of red, blue, and yellow cake base*
- *White frosting (vanilla or cheese cream)*
- *Superhero emblem decorations (store-bought or homemade)*
- *Edible gold stars (for decoration)*
- *Cake pop sticks*

Instructions:

- Prepare a batch of red, blue, and yellow cake pops using a basic vanilla cake recipe with coloring. Mix the white frosting with the cake crumbs.
- Shape the mixture into small balls and place them on a baking sheet. Insert with pop sticks.
- Dip each pop into the white frosting, allowing it to serve as the base for the emblem, then attach superhero emblem decorations.
- Sprinkle with edible gold stars for that power burst effect.

Minion Mayhem Banana Pops

Making Time: 2 hours – 24 Cake Pops

Ingredients:

- 1 batch of yellow banana-flavored cake base
- Yellow frosting (vanilla or cream cheese with yellow food coloring)
- Edible candy eyes
- Black icing or candy melts (for decoration)
- Cake pop sticks

Instructions:

- Prepare a batch of yellow banana-flavored cake using a banana-flavored vanilla cake recipe. Mix the yellow frosting with the cake crumbs.
- Shape the mixture into small balls and place them on a baking sheet, then insert with cake pop sticks.
- Dip each pop into the yellow frosting, then attach edible candy eyes and create minion overalls and goggles using black icing or melted black candy melts. Set and serve!

TIPS, TRICKS, TROUBLESHOOTING

In the world of cake pops, every baker, from novice to experts, can benefit from a little extra knowledge and insight. This section is your go-to resource for enhancing your cake pop skills, overcoming common pitfalls, and exploring advanced techniques that will take your creations to the next level.

You will learn essential tips for proper storage and transportation of cake pops, ensuring they maintain their taste and appearance. You'll uncover the most common mistakes that can occur during the cake pop-making process, helping you steer clear of culinary mishaps. Additionally, we'll introduce advanced decorating techniques that will transform your cake pops into edible masterpieces. Happy baking and decorating!

Storing Cake Pops

Once the cake pops are made, they usually have to wait for a few hours or a day so that that birthday, holiday, or a party comes along! So, what is the secret to storing them properly?

Simply store the cake pops in an airtight container if you want to eat them within a day or two. Before storing them it's crucial to ensure your pops have cooled down entirely. If they're still warm when stored, moisture can build up inside the container and cause the cake pops to become soggy or even fall apart. We don't want that, do we?

106

Cake pops may be kept fresh for longer if they are individually wrapped. You can use plastic or cellophane wrap. This not only helps retain moisture but also prevents the pops from absorbing any odors or flavors from the surrounding environment. Make sure to keep them out of sun and health though.

Opt for an airtight container that is appropriately sized for the number of cakes you want to store. This minimizes air exposure and helps maintain their freshness. Using clear containers can also make it easy to see the decorations and designs that you have worked so hard on.

We want to avoid that so that it does not ruin your decorations, but if you need to stack the pops on top of each other in the container, separate the layers with parchment paper. This prevents them from sticking together and might help keep your decorations in place.

If you intend to store your cake pops for an extended period, use the freezer. Wrap each cake pop individually in plastic wrap to prevent freezer burn. Then, place them in an airtight container. Make sure there's a little space between the cake pops, and they shouldn't touch one another directly. It's essential to freeze the cake pops as quickly as possible after they've cooled to maintain their moisture. If you let them sit at room temperature for an extended period before freezing, they can start to dry out and they will not be any good.

Always label the container with the date you froze the cake pops. This will help you keep track of their freshness and use them within a reasonable time frame. When you're ready to enjoy your frozen cake pops, take them out of the freezer and let them thaw in the refrigerator or at room temperature. Slow thawing prevents condensation, which can affect the cake pop's texture and appearance.

Avoid storing cake pops in the refrigerator if possible. The humidity inside the refrigerator can cause the cake pops to absorb moisture, making them soggy and affecting their flavor. Storing them at room temperature or in the freezer is generally the best approach for maintaining their quality.

Transporting Cake Pops

Transporting your beautifully crafted cake pops safely is a crucial step in ensuring they arrive at their destination in perfect condition. Whether you're bringing them to a party, delivering them as a gift, or selling them at an event, here are some essential tips to help you master the art of cake pop transportation.

- **Choose the Right Container**

Select a container that's both practical and secure. Consider the size of the container and the number of pieces you're transporting. Cake pop containers or boxes designed specifically for this purpose are ideal, as they come with slots or holes to hold each pop in place. Ensure your container has a secure lid or seal to keep the cake pops safe during travel. If you're using a cardboard box, tape the lid securely to prevent it from accidentally opening.

- **Secure the Pops**

If your container doesn't have built-in slots, use foam blocks, floral foam, or even rice to anchor the cake pops in an upright position. This prevents them from moving around and colliding during transit, preserving their appearance.

- **Layer with Parchment Paper**

Place parchment paper between layers of cake pops, especially if you're stacking them in a container. This simple step prevents the pops from sticking to one another and messing up their decorations.

- **Keep Them Cool**

If the weather is warm, consider using a cooler bag or insulated container to maintain a cool temperature during transportation. Cake pops can become soft or melt in high temperatures, so keep them out of heat!

- **Do not Overcrowd**

Don't pack too many pops into a single container. Overcrowding can lead to damage, and the decorations might smudge. Leave some space to maintain their visual appeal. Before heading out, gently shake or tilt the container to make sure the cake pops are stable and won't shift during transport.

- **Secure the Container**

During transportation, keep the container level and secure. If you're driving, place it on a flat surface in the car, away from any sharp turns or sudden stops. If you're traveling on foot or public transport, hold the container steady to prevent any accidents.

Transporting cake pops can be stress-free and successful with the right preparation and attention to detail. Enjoy the satisfaction of sharing your cake pop creations wherever you go!

Common Mistakes & How to Fix Them

Even the most seasoned cake pop enthusiasts can make the occasional misstep. Let's explore some common mistakes that can happen during the cake pop-making process and learn how to fix them like a pro.

- **My Cake is Crumbling**

Overmixing the cake crumbs with frosting can lead to a crumbly texture that's challenging to shape into cake pops. Add frosting gradually and stop once the mixture reaches a dough-like consistency. If it's too crumbly, add a bit more frosting until it's easier to work with.

- **My Cake Pops are Soggy**

This usually means too much frosting. To salvage overly moist cake pops, add more cake crumbs and mix until the texture becomes firmer. This should balance the moisture content.

- **My Cake Pops are Falling Off Sticks**

Probably the coating is too heavy, or they haven't been secured properly. To prevent that, ensure the sticks are inserted deep enough into the pops. Dip the sticks into the coating before inserting them to create a better bond and tap off excess coating to prevent an overly thick layer.

- **My Coating is Cracking**

Your coating is probably too thick, which can lead to unsightly cracks.

Thin the coating with a small amount of vegetable oil or paramount crystals. This will result in smoother, more even coating.

- **My Coating is Dripping**

The opposite problem from a thick coating: your coating is too thin. To thicken the coating, gently reheat it and stir in more melted chocolate or candy melts until you achieve the desired consistency.

- **Decorations Won't Stick**

Sprinkles, edible pearls, or other decorations might not stick properly to the cake pops. It's essential to apply them immediately after dipping the cake pops before the coating sets. This ensures they adhere securely.

- **I Can't Shape them Evenly**

Cake pops can develop uneven shapes if they aren't rolled into smooth balls or if the coating is applied haphazardly. So, take your time shaping the cake pops into round, smooth balls. When applying the coating, rotate the cake pop and tap off excess coating to create an even, uniform finish.

Remember, making mistakes is all part of the learning process. By identifying common cake pop errors, you'll improve your cake pop-making skills and create beautiful, delicious treats every time.

Decoration Tips and Advanced Techniques

Elevating your cake pop game to a professional level involves mastering decoration techniques and exploring advanced methods. Here are some tips and insights to help you create stunning cake pops that leave a lasting impression:

- To achieve intricate designs, consider using piping bags with fine tips to apply details like delicate swirls, fine lines, or intricate patterns.
- Create a marbling effect by combining different colors of candy melts or chocolate on the cake pop's surface. Swirl the colors while the coating is still wet to achieve a visually captivating result.
- Invest in an airbrush kit to add professional-grade color and shading to your cake pops. Airbrushing allows for smooth gradients and intricate details with minimal effort.

- Add a touch of glamour to your cake pops by using edible metallic dust or edible gold or silver leaf. These accents can transform your pops into elegant confectionery art.

- Experiment with edible image sheets or edible ink markers to transfer intricate designs, logos, or photographs onto your cake pops. This is an excellent option for custom orders or themed events.

- Create texture on your cake pops by rolling them in crushed nuts, sprinkles, or edible glitter while the coating is still wet. The added texture provides a visually appealing contrast.

- Craft fondant shapes or figures to adorn your cake pops. Fondant allows for intricate detailing and adds a professional touch to your creations.

- Brush embroidery involves using a fine paintbrush to create delicate, lacy patterns on the cake pop's surface. This technique is particularly charming for floral designs.

- Experiment with multi-layered cake pops by inserting smaller cake pops into larger ones, creating a unique and visually striking treat.

- Surprise your recipients with hidden designs inside your cake pops. Whether it's a vibrant color or a hidden shape, the "reveal" can be a delightful and unexpected touch.

- Master geometric shapes on your cake pops by using edible markers or colored coatings to create intricate patterns, such as triangles, diamonds, or chevrons.

Achieving professional-level decoration often comes down to patience and a steady hand. Take your time, and practice intricate designs to enhance your cake pop artistry. It can be a rewarding journey for those who want to take their creations to the next level. Remember, practice makes perfect, so don't be discouraged if it takes time to master these skills.

CONCLUSION

Congratulations on reaching the end of your delightful cake pop journey! You've embarked on a sweet and creative adventure, exploring a world of flavors, colors, and endless possibilities.

Cake pops are not just desserts; they are tiny, edible works of art. The beauty of cake pops lies not only in their deliciousness but also in the joy they bring to those who enjoy them. With your newfound skills and boundless creativity, you have the power to create happiness, one cake pop at a time.

Let your imagination run wild, experimenting with flavors, decorations, and themes. Share your creations with friends and family, spreading smiles and making moments even more special.

Always remember that each cake pop you make is a small masterpiece, a testament to your culinary passion. Whether you're crafting them for celebrations, special occasions, or just because, know that the joy you share through your creations is a gift to be cherished.

The world of cake pops is boundless, and your journey is far from over. Continue exploring, innovating, and delighting taste buds. We wish you endless success in your cake pop endeavors and countless moments of happiness in the kitchen.

We are sure the pops will bring joy and creativity to your life!

Made in the USA
Columbia, SC
30 November 2024

48010709R00065